Views from the Lanai

poems by

Patricia Barry

Finishing Line Press
Georgetown, Kentucky

Views from the Lanai

This chapbook is dedicated to my husband, Robert, with profound gratitude for our love and our inspiring daily journey together, which brought us to Florida and ultimately led to the poetry herein.

ACKNOWLEDGMENTS

My deep thanks go to my virtual writing group, a talented team of authors.
This chapbook would not have been possible without their feedback, candor,
and encouragement. They are Andrea Simon, for her inspiration and editing
expertise—she was a motivating force in bringing this chapbook to fruition;
Pamela Leggett, for her insights on the shape and narrative of this book;
Sanna Stanley, for her reflections clarifying my thinking in some of these
poems; Jane Gardner, for her perceptive suggestions and proofreading;
Katherine Kirkpatrick, for her detailed comments and thoughtful statements
about the emotional arc of this chapbook; and Stephanie Cowell, for
bringing her novelist's eye and attention to this collection.

And I am wholeheartedly grateful to my sister, Kathy McMahon, my
sounding board through several drafts of each poem—her love, support, and
wisdom are apparent in this chapbook from beginning to end.

Publisher: Leah Huete de Maines
Editor: Christen Kincaid
Cover Art: Andrea Simon, https://www.andreasimon.net
Author Photos: Brynn Colmer, Just a Wrinkle in Time Photography
Cover Design: Elizabeth Maines McCleavy

Order online: www.finishinglinepress.com
also available on amazon.com

Author inquiries and mail orders:
Finishing Line Press
PO Box 1626
Georgetown, Kentucky 40324
USA

Contents

PART ONE: BEGINNING

MOURNING DOVE

The distant cooing of the mourning dove
sounds as if it's inside me—
insistent, rhythmic, soft and low,
resonating deep within my chest
in the vicinity of my
usually tranquil heart.

The cooing is muffled,
like my thoughts trying to
escape through time;
so many memories crowd me while
a new life calls to me.

Suddenly my poetry
breaks through the surface,
making music only I can hear
against a green landscape
bounded by a line of trees
empty of birds
where the singing must be
my own.

TABLEAU

This afternoon I'm watching a large egret
fly over the pond, settle on the fairway, and
stand completely still for a moment,
a tableau in white and grey captured
in a green velvet frame.
The egret starts walking—
like a Limoges figurine come to life
among lost golf balls—
a procelain memory that refuses to stay
on the safety of the shelf.

Suddenly a noisy, grass-green lawn tractor
enters the scene, shattering the silence,
and the startled egret flies off,
its vast wingspan soaring out of sight
as the mower finishes its job.

Then two golf carts appear
and the golfers get out to take their shots—
a pastel of light blue shirts and white shorts,
the carts gleaming alabaster and golf clubs shining.

If only the egret had stayed to complete that canvas,
it would have been all the more beautiful, I think.
But I know a memory cannot compete
with the fully lived present;
that possibility had fled with the egret.

I'm left with golfers playing their game
in the fading four o'clock sun,
unaware of the shadows they cast
or the fragile, fleeting beauty of a moment ago.

THE POND

The pond behind our house
has a current this windy afternoon;
it swiftly courses
to the sandy shore two backyards down.
The pond is white as I look south,
silver as I look north, and
fairly sparkling in the moving waters
nearest our lanai.
I want to capture its beauty, its message,
but it keeps changing—
don't ponder the present,
it seems to say,
or here I am for you
to catch the meaning of
light on water—
one moment flowing into the next,
heedless of me and my pen.

I must let the current go
as it continues past,
the pond emptying its
essence onto the gravelly soil
where the heron waits motionlessly
while the white duck, like me,
hurriedly picks its way
toward that sustenance
along the water's edge.

FLORIDA INTERLOPER

Did the closeness of the sun to the earth,
its arc across the Florida sky,
lead to the stubby beak of the native hawk or
burn to white the long tail feathers of the
light-colored osprey?
I could believe
the climate or the region
made them that way,
so exotic and inescapable,
as foreign to this
New York transplant
as the palm trees are.

But I don't know how to coexist with—
let alone accept—
the proximate sun, frond, and feather;
all at once
they fill my front yard
on this oppressively hot
April morning.
How can I fit into
this teeming tropical place
when even the stiff grass
resists my footsteps?

Starting back inside,
I discover the familiar
white-and-red azaleas
near my front door
are welcoming me
like an old New York friend
to an early Florida spring.

RARE BIRD

The woodpecker comes to our backyard only rarely,
showing its regal red head briefly
among the magnolia branches,
dropping to attach itself to the tree trunk and start pecking.
Today it holds itself in position,
completely in control, magisterial and still, then
decides to fly away, directly to the dense stand of trees
beyond the golf course.

Its flight is measured and sure, barely picking up speed
over the pond as it takes off, and
not slowed to look for its noble reflection.
No, the woodpecker does not alter its pace
above the soft green terrain or study its shadow,
but keeps a consistent momentum in the air,
focused only on its mission,
knowing it need not hurry nor tarry.
It moves forward steadily, relentlessly, like time itself.

The woodpecker answers a call I cannot hear;
is it from the tree it nests in or the forest,
its mate or the abundance of birds in the woods
looking for their leader?

Take my questions with you, Resolute Bird,
and leave your flight plan here.
A forest of my own calls me away from the window—
thickets of poems and prayers propel me,
one leading to another—
a steady hand, a willing heart,
where do I land first?

THE ALLIGATOR

An alligator suns itself on the pond bank
bordering the fairway out back.
It's unmoved by the golf carts that come near it,
changing its position only as it suits itself—
now facing east, slanted toward the water—
until a golfer comes too close
and it drops back into the pond
rather than deal with him.

I am that alligator,
taking my time to soak up the sun around me,
staying and overstaying where I may not be welcome
until someone gets too close and I,
prickly creature, have to shift away,
drop out of sight awhile.
I have not yet learned the art of
peaceful coexistence,
taking my leave in various ways until
the threat is neutralized
and it's safe to emerge
from the pond of my longing again.

ASH WEDNESDAY

The bright white ibis appear in flocks on the far bank
of the pond behind our lanai,
new arrivals like the ashes smudged on my forehead today.
I sit watching those birds for a moment as they industriously
poke the ground with their long beaks and
jut their heads up, as if chewing,
digesting what they've found.
It's almost as if they're talking to each other as they go
about their searching and eating,
sociable in their groupings, together in all.
They include me in their company
as one strays nearby and passes me.
Soon they will leave for literally greener pastures
than the jagged, muddy apron of the pond shore.

For now I enjoy their company and think of them as
pecking away at my faults,
unearthing them, bringing them to light and,
blessedly, carrying them away
as Lent begins.

UPHEAVALS

There's a power shovel digging three sand traps
on the golf course out back this afternoon,
the bunkers being dug deeper and wider
while the golfers play through.
I see some players putting on a precipice
above the largest and most gaping of the three pits.

Those bunkers remind me of the emptied home
we left behind in New York.
My husband, sister, and I forcefully scooped out its contents,
encompassing three generations, two floors, a basement,
sub-basement, and attic.
We brought a small fraction of our possessions here—
mostly family pictures, beloved books, stereo equipment,
trusty kitchen tools, summer clothes, and some furniture—
after a winnowing process I would not care to repeat.

But there is always more to let go of—my fear of
not fitting in with those around me and
not adapting to my new life in Florida.
I speak to my neighbors, usually on my way to get mail,
about water filtration or hurricane-proof windows.
My forays into the outskirts of our lives sometimes cross paths
with ibis and crows, and hold the possibility of friendship later on.

At times I'm like the little blue heron that strayed
into our front yard yesterday, away from feeding grounds
in the back and its companions, the egret, crane, and osprey.
Suddenly feeling lost, I catch myself and go on,
teetering across a pitted green landscape,
trying to find my way home.

THE GREAT WHITE EGRET

The great white egret appears this cold morning
on the pond dock opposite me.
It is folded into itself,
turned to allow the sun to warm its back,
glowing brighter from the rays being absorbed.

When I look up again, it's already flown
across the pond to our backyard,
on the slant by the base of the bank,
watching the water with its neck extended,
now pulled back, its mouth
moving in a kind of prayer or anticipation of prey.

As the egret saunters out of my view,
I realize I am the one contracted into myself,
longing to find and gather in what's necessary—
hope and courage to carry on in this time of virus;
faith, love, and a stronger sense of self and mission—
then, warmed by a gracious sun, keep walking.
And so I begin to stretch and stride
to meet what the day brings.

BUTTERFLY AND TOAD, DREAMING

After the contractor replaced the screens
on the pool enclosure yesterday,
he pointed out the orange butterfly
above us—it was bumping against the mesh at the peak
of the rafters.

He said that he had saved the butterfly from being crushed
when he swapped out that section of the screening;
it hadn't flown away during the entire process.

Today the butterfly tells me it's caught in this life,
making the most of the space the contractor gave it,
trying to transcend the roof over its head—
only habit keeping it from going higher.
Drifting toward me for a moment,
the butterfly says it wants to go as high as it can
and know what and when to escape.

I turn; something else is moving,
wedged in the door latch to the enclosure.
I approach it and see a pale brown toad,
now very still, imploring me
with its large, yellow-brown eyes.
I quickly free it and place it on a nearby bush outside—
it may have jumped from there to the open door yesterday,
becoming stuck in its not-so-short,
hopeful hop to a better place.

All I can say is freedom is not a disposable dream
or easily squelched—and so I ask myself,
where do I want to go and can I get there
even if I am an orange butterfly or a beige toad?

THE THREE DEER

Three deer came to the fairway today.
Suddenly they were across from my husband and me,
perhaps fifty yards from a group of golfers
who did not approach them—
two adult deer and a baby one, standing still,
looking toward us into the lanai.
The adults looked away
but the fawn continued gazing,
and would still be there
except that its parents bounded away;
the fawn followed,
heading to the far end of the pond.

What was the young deer looking at—
me, my husband, the lanai—
how far did that new gaze penetrate our defenses,
our starting-over lives here, our welcoming hearts?
Or did its scrutiny stay on the surface, determining
by some scanning instinct or imprint that we were
friend or foe by our silhouettes—
worth a second look, I hope,
sometime soon.

PART TWO: ADAPTING

OUT OF THE FOG

Dense fog, early morning—
I barely see the large heron across the pond
through the mist of my own concerns.
It's standing on the small concrete landing
at the shoreline, a place
to get its bearings in low visibility.
I watch the heron watch the water,
then the pond bank,
looking for something.
It peers out
toward me.

But my thoughts are faraway,
in a Northeast blizzard of snow, ice and
worry about my far-flung family being safe.
How clearly, how far, can the heron see
through the weather of memory and droplets of fog?
We both hunch over, concentrating,
then straighten up, alert.
I am the only other sign of life right now.

This morning was made for us
to watch each other lift our heads
from under this heavy blanket of haze
until the heron beats its wings in its flying walk,
dispelling murk and uncertainty with
each flap and flutter
so we can both come into focus
and start the day.

OUR NEIGHBOR'S TREETOP

This morning is going fast, speeding past me as I rise
and go to the nook at the back of our house.
The shadows of treetops appear on the pond bank
and disappear quickly as the sun races westward,
already over our roof.
The dark angular outline of our neighbor's tree has
softened into the curves this day will throw at me,
that I must be ready for—
as that treetop's shadow sinks into the water
where I cannot see it anymore,
a Rorschach test conducted from memory.
All my wits about me now, I try to discern
what I must hold onto as the sun traverses the sky.

Hang onto friendliness despite the coronavirus
around us—
try to be neighborly today;
let go of the conversation I was too busy
to have yesterday with our potential friend
across the street while I was chasing squirrels
out of the garage.
Some golfers are rushing in their carts
to the green beyond the pond and
a white egret sails over
to the water's edge nearest me.
I have some catching up to do
and second chances to take
before the shadows gather again.

DEGREES OF SEPARATION

The birds in our backyard are active today.
A little blue heron paced and stretched its wings
just outside the screen enclosure,
then headed away from where we sat
in the kitchen nook with our tea, going on
the computer, worrying about the virus—
only looking up when there's a commotion
of feathers outside.
A large crane flies across the pond and
heads south right over the lanai.
The crane, bright white, has a wide wingspan and
glides gracefully, pumping its wings only once,
then travels to the other end of the pond.
My husband, Robert, says it's as if the birds
were inside the lanai.
That's just outside our nook where we are
keeping social distance
between us and the birds.

But today, I am weary of it all—
the lanai screen, the glass window in the nook,
the several degrees of separation.
There is a greater closeness I need right now,
when we all must pull together.
Nature is calling *my* nature to bring down the divide,
close the gap between me and where the crane flies
and the little blue heron paces.
They remind me to look around and up,
to be mindful that life does go on despite the virus
and its terrible toll.
I'm leaving the nook today,
venturing into our backyard.

AN OLD-FASHIONED RAIN

It's an old-fashioned rain that
wakes me up on Sunday,
the kind with quiet thunder
that gently rolls into my consciousness,
so that I don't know
what awakened me early
until I start to listen to a sound
that feels so long ago.
It's not the crashing noise of the severe storms
here in Florida that jolts me awake
in the middle of the night.
No, it's the steady, soft sound of rain and storm
that starts to rock me back to sleep
in its gentle rhythms, moderate wind, and
ways of holding me together
under the quilt with you.

Later I get up to get ready
to take our dog, Cody, outside.
The day has begun and the prospect of coffee
drives me to the kitchen nook—
and on this old-fashioned Sunday morning,
I taste a cup of fresh contentment
before heading out into the welcome rain.

COUNTING DOVES

Like a child's counting game,
five mourning doves
march along the base of the lanai,
all in a row
pecking the ground as they go,
not breaking stride.
They emerge one by one
from behind the raised rim of the pool
as if it were a vaudeville curtain,
their rumpled feathers bearing witness
to a rough-and-tumble world,
the pounding of last night's rain—
from that chaos a neat chorus line
forms this morning.
They round the corner
to feed under the hedge
and collect themselves in private
before their next appearance
under the new day's sun.

SUNSET

An egret flew to the edge of the pond bank
across from our lanai.
It touched down in a path of light,

silvery sparkles rippling the water
fanning out from the shore toward me.
The egret rested long enough for a moment of grace

and flew away, the sunset trailing behind.
The sun still setting, the pond continued to shine,
energy coming to a point where now a

heron sets down upon the bank,
and the light spreads out toward me again,
in a locus of life on the water

that the egret left for me
unexpectedly.

PART THREE: CALLING IT HOME

CALL IT HOME

When the sun is too much, I wear sunscreen,
sandals, and capris like Florida natives—
or retreat inside for a while as they do.
When the palm trees close in, I know it's time to
prune and pick up the fronds.
I call my neighbor for water issues, and
I know to turn on the pump and open the spigot
when the pool level is too high.
The stiff grass accepts my footsteps better
when it's short.
And when the osprey swoops low overhead,
I duck a little and keep walking.

Yes, I had to adjust my expectations and myself
to this environment—at first, as if I were wallpaper
without glue, I tried to cover all surfaces at once,
the angles where I'd hoped to fit in, not sticking there
and thinking that every bit of space was already
taken up by a pattern of sun, frond and feather.
I had to change, piece by piece, take time to adapt
and be open to meet nature halfway at least.
I share its world, after all, and through my experiences
and writing, am gaining insights into how to live here.

Now I find I see things as they are.
Elements that seemed daunting can be accommodated
and learned from: walks by the muddy pond bank,
a microcosm of life, grow into a reservoir of wisdom;
birds inspire me with their flights and struggles; and
front-yard talks with neighbors go beyond the weather.
I have come to accept what is all around me, give thanks
for its beauty, live with it every day, and call it home.

THIS CLEAR MORNING

When I took our dog, Cody, out this morning
the freshness of the air enveloped us right away
as we rushed to his favorite spot by the front hedge.
The sky was sheer blue, almost transparent,
"a view of heaven," I said aloud,
glancing at the sun.
It was not yet directly overhead,
the heat was bearable,
and the light was softer than it would be later.

When we went inside, I saw the pond out back
was like a mirror—
there was a stillness despite golfers already on the green
lining up their shots, as if in a movie without sound,
a story told in freeze frame.
The pond reflected
their game, some palm fronds stirring, and
two crows flying by.

Then the golfers and crows were gone.
A white-and-black tern flew over the pond.
No one stopped for long, all casting
their reflections under heaven
this clear morning.

GATEKEEPER

The pond water is rippling wildly and
the sky is stone-cold grey this early morning.
No one is around except me and a vigilant gatekeeper—
the brown osprey who perches on the topmost
corner of the lanai.

I can see he's on guard, in control, and
willing to face danger—whatever sustains
his mighty heart and solid frame, those
stoic yellow eyes, and that heroic profile—beak uplifted.

Then a flame-feathered cardinal lands in a nearby
tree and sings her offering to the osprey;
she bounds to the far magnolia and
he follows close behind.
Within minutes, the osprey returns alone
to stand watch again—looking out toward the
threatening sky and the fast-moving pond, the way
I'm facing.

Out of sight among dense magnolia leaves,
did this noble bird, guardian of the gate of the heart,
grant the cardinal access to his heart's desire—his
innermost wishes to protect, keep safe, and even to love?

I believe he returned to his post satisfied and
opened his heart again, this time to confront the
imminent storm with me and quell the fear in my heart.

Suddenly the osprey flies away, to meet and defeat
a coming disaster— or chase someone else's dream.

BEYOND ARTHRITIS

The slate grey heron, colored by rain,
stands with its wings outstretched this clear, still morning.
After yesterday's full-on storm,
and the rain of three previous days measured by my
overflowing pool,
it's time for the heron to dry out those
impressive, wide wings—sails unfurled and immovable,
ready to catch the wind
when it will come again.

Moving unsteadily to the lanai in my new orthopedic boot,
I watch the heron on and off throughout this afternoon;
it's in a different location each time I look up—
on the fairway at the edge of a foursome,
then closer to the pond shore,
ultimately on the small concrete pad on the pond.
The heron's wings look like two static flags held open
not by the wind but by their own design and power—
as if planted on the moon—
or like an emblem to wear as a brooch on my lapel,
to celebrate the day when I decide to be more open,
to dry out from the soppy storms of life that
black out the television and my outlook
with complications from arthritis flares and
conflicting medical and fixit-guy appointments.

Now I see the heron has flown away.
I too want to be free of my landing pad—
my arthritic stomping grounds—
and stride swiftly under drier skies and soft winds,
with the healing that comes from unfolding my wings
and being ready, after a time,
to fly again.

GARBAGE DAY

God is the ultimate garbage man.
His all-encompassing forgiveness
seeps into the corners of my life today,
where I hold past mistakes, old conflicts,
clothes that are too small, medical complications,
and our dog, Cara's, lost rawhide bones—
and hauls them away, freeing me.
He tells me those things and their weighty
significance are gone; they don't matter and can't
hold me back anymore from the goodness I owe myself,
the plans I want to make for me as I am now—
hobbled by an arthritis flare.

Cara is God's close second in the garbage game—
carrying away the pens I don't use, the empty
pages of an old pad, and the ragged first draft of this poem.
I'm not quick enough to snatch them from her as she
toys with me; she won't give them back
unless I bribe her.
She taunts me—how important are they to you;
what do you really want to do with them, now?

I tell Cara to hand them over: I'm opening up
to catch the muse again—
and let fly new ideas and still-hopeful ones—
with reclaimed, chewed pens and ripped pads today.
Time to celebrate garbage day—
a letting-go, self-forgiving, self-accepting day—
with recycled joy.
Join me at the curb,
dancing in my orthopedic boot.

ACCEPTANCE

What does it mean to coexist
with ospreys, egrets, ibis and crows
in this gradually familiar place?
I want to interact with them
but it's not as if they come
and rest on my shoulder or
take seed from my fingers.
They look me in the eye only rarely,
when they're on the ground, walking
in the front yard,
or approaching me before flying past.
We meet in each other's periphery—
the edge of our lanai or the lawn—
their eagle-eyes out for something
more like food or danger.

And so we coexist in our parallel lives.
I see the osprey protecting me at its post
on our lanai, and
the egret diving over the pond to show me
how to move lyrically.
The crow and ibis sound warnings
when the storm approaches.
What I see as their courage and missions
teach me to be spirit-led into
companionship and respect.
In this tropical heat all around me,
coexistence moves imperceptibly into the
velvety warmth of acceptance.

THE SURFACE OF FAVORABLE THINGS

Praying and searching for joy this morning,
I find it across the pond from our lanai—
sprinkles of bright yellow on the bank catch my eye.
I squint—are they dandelions or buttercups?—
but it doesn't matter which;
either one signals a beautiful neglect
on the edge of the manicured green fairway,
inches from the rushing pond.
The sun is at such an angle that
the rippling current cannot contain itself—
it casts sparkles onto the bank,
where the reflection hurries equally swiftly
among the vivid yellow flowers all along the shore.

I never saw a sight like this before,
a sign to keep going in circumstances as I find them—
keep writing my life as it surges past,
see its surprising beauty
despite writer's block,
caregiving pressures, and
pounds to lose—
let myself be mesmerized, even changed,
by the surface of favorable things.

Now I'm racing to catch up with myself
on the solid ground of the shoreline,
my strides keeping pace with the pond in the sun,
while wild gold blossoms on the glinting path
reflect my joy and gratitude—
no questions asked anymore—
this unexpected, magnificent morning.

IN THE LAND OF HIGH CEILINGS

In the land of high ceilings
I was too used to not looking up so much.
Although my view here is not bounded by
a low ceiling closing in on me as it was
in New York, at first I took for granted
the freedom to breathe deeply the greater
volume of air in our Florida living room.
Creature of habit, I had learned well
what it was to look straight ahead at
the next thing in front of me to do—wash dishes;
walk our dog, Cody; cook broccoli mac and cheese—
and applied those lessons here,
seeing only the immediate present:
duties, yes—but now

there's the osprey in our yard,
pond waters streaming outside,
golfers on the green across the pond.
Watching and writing from the lanai,
I found the natural world
opened up for me
on a level it never had before
and became my home, too.

Now I see the blue sky
as boundless, changing, the landscape
of white clouds anything but static.
The world pivots.
I lift my gaze again and
take a deep breath—clouds on a roll,
shifting southerly right now—
getting on with my new life.

A SURPRISE APPEARANCE

Today is the big day when I get my photo taken
for the back cover of this chapbook of poetry
about my adapting to life in Florida through
native-bird encounters, mostly in my backyard.
When Brynn, of Just a Wrinkle in Time Photography
(yes, a Madeleine L'Engle admirer like me),
arrives, we head directly out the lanai door, toward
a magnolia tree, quiet pond, clear blue sky, and
onto the lush green grass.

Brynn suddenly asks, "is that an osprey?"—I look
above the pond at my old friend, the little blue heron.
I tell Brynn the heron has chosen to make a surprise
appearance out of the pages of my chapbook.
The bird sets down on the shore, starts to approach
us, and then stops inside the photo frame.
Brynn, inspired, tells me her lense captured
the heron and me together.
The heron vanishes as soon as we turn away;
it had stayed just long enough to give its approval—
no, its blessing—on these proceedings.

Within the sweep of that benediction, we go where
the spirit takes us, down low on the lanai stoop and
over into our neighbor's yard where a stand of trees
and an orange bush beckon.
The lanai calls us for final shots of nature's favor.
The photo gallery will arrive by next Monday,
Brynn promises—the heron and I can hardly wait
until grace descends again.

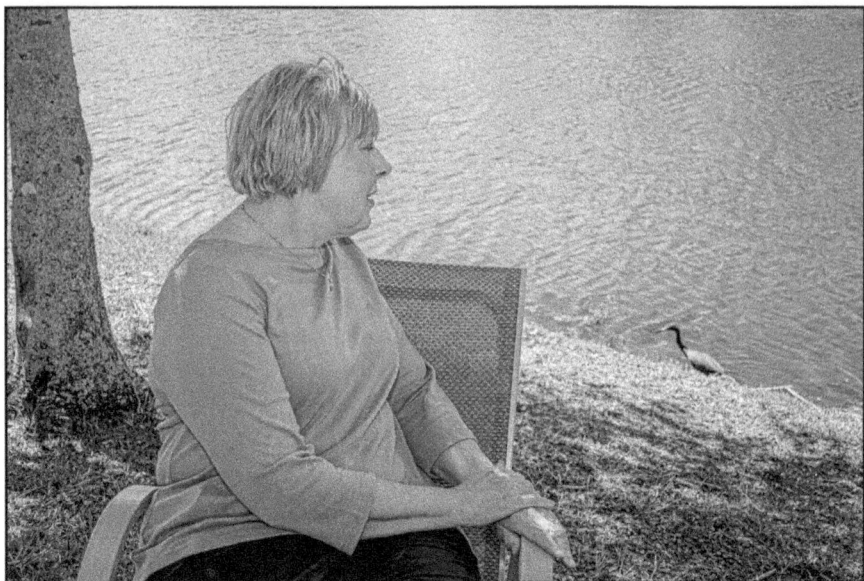

Patricia Barry was born and raised in Connecticut. She has a B.A. in English from Central Connecticut State University and a J.D. from St. John's University School of Law. For thirty-three years in New York City, her law practice encompassed writing appellate briefs in the workers' compensation field. As time went on, she studied writing with noted author Madeleine L'Engle, who became her mentor. Then she joined a long-term writing group that blossomed from Madeleine's workshops, and began to write poetry.

In 2018, Patricia and her husband, Robert, an electrical engineer, retired from New York to Florida. What could have been a familiar retirement story took an unexpected turn—a poetic turn with an avian twist. Finding herself in Palm Coast, Patricia discovered a new world from her lanai. This screened-in porch under the extended back roofline of her house contains a pool and looks out onto a pond, some backyard trees, and a golf course across the pond. The lanai turned out to be an excellent vantage point from which she could view herons, ospreys, hawks, eagles, egrets, ibis, woodpeckers, crows and the occasional alligator and deer. Wildlife now surrounded her as never before in her daily life. The Florida birds were exotic to her; they sparked her curiosity and she began writing about them and her ever-changing landscape.

As the pandemic kept her at home, the native birds and wildlife became an important link to the outside world beyond the usual run of doctors' visits, grocery deliveries, and takeout. She became more acclimated to Florida through her views from the lanai. Motivated by her writing group—which had begun to meet virtually—she started to write each week, calling the series of poems, "Today's Delights." And so evolved this collection of poetry, in which the alligator, deer, butterfly, and toad appear along with birds, people, and her German shepherd dogs: first, Cody, and now, Cara.

Nature opened her heart, mind, and senses in each encounter with wildlife, especially the native birds. In this chapbook, she shares the resulting insights into where she is in life and how she adapted to an entirely new environment.

The birds continue to inspire her with their spontaneity, spirited flights, and interactions. In the process of writing about the wildlife in Florida, she found, and still finds, surprising examples of perseverance, resilience, beauty, and the quest for freedom. Her hope is that this collection may inspire and uplift others in their daily lives.

Patricia's poetry has appeared in *St. Anthony Messenger; The Palm Coast Observer;* and *Of Poets and Poetry,* a publication of the Florida State Poets Association.

www.ingramcontent.com/pod-product-compliance
Lightning Source LLC
Chambersburg PA
CBHW022047080426
42734CB00009B/1273